MOON MILK

MOON MILK

MILK

EASY RECIPES FOR PEACEFUL SLEEP

ANNI DAULTER

WITH JESSICA BOOTH AND ALEXIS DONAHUE

Photographs by *Megan Elizondo*

GIBBS SMITH
TO ENRICH AND INSPIRE HUMANKIND

First Edition
24 23 22 21 20   5 4 3 2 1

Text © 2020 Anni Daulter
Photographs © 2020 Megan Elizondo

Published by
Gibbs Smith
P.O. Box 667
Layton, Utah 84041

1.800.835.4993 orders
www.gibbs-smith.com

Designed by Rita Sowins / Sowins Design
Contributing writers Jessica Booth and Alexis Donahue
Printed and bound in Hong Kong
Gibbs Smith books are printed on paper produced from sustainable PEFC-
certified forest/controlled wood source. Learn more at www.pefc.org.

Library of Congress Cataloging-in-Publication Data

Names: Daulter, Anni, author. | Elizondo, Megan, photographer.
Title: Moon milk : easy recipes for peaceful sleep / Anni Daulter ;
photographs by Megan Elizondo.
Description: First edition. | Layton : Gibbs Smith, [2020] |
Identifiers: LCCN 2019036072 | ISBN 9781423654483 (hardcover) |
ISBN 9781423654490 (epub)
Subjects: LCSH: Beverages. | LCGFT: Cookbooks.
Classification: LCC TX815 .D24 2020 | DDC 641.2—dc23
LC record available at https://lccn.loc.gov/2019036072

TO OUR FAMILIES AND FRIENDS WHO SUPPORTED
AND LOVED OUR MOONALICIOUS VISION!

CONTENTS

Acknowledgments

We would like to thank all those who appreciate the magic of the moon and all her wondrous gifts—and the following folks for their moon milk inspiration:

Lesley Gilbert for her moon-inspired water color art, and for sharing herbs from her apothecary, Sacred Spaces Co.; Megan Elizondo of Nutmeg Photography for her constant positive vibes and beautiful images; and Leigh Lamitola for supporting our vision and helping it come to life.

THE
MILKY WAY

WHY MOON MILKS?

Moon Milks are a soft sip of nurturing for your body, mind, and soul. They gently soothe jangled nerves, calm bedtime jitters, and unwind those internal springs that so often keep us from the quiet respite that evening offers. Some of the milk recipes are a playful walk down the lane of sweet childhood memories, a favorite cereal, a moment lost in a daydream. Others contain colorful adaptogens, a class of herbs known to help balance energy and nourish tired adrenals. These touchstones to our senses help us call up the inner peace and tranquility of those quiet moments.

MILKY BASICS & HOW TO'S

CHOOSING MILKS

There is a whole wide world of milk options out there today. If you are concerned over allergens from grains, nuts, or dairy, feel free to swap our recommendation for your favorite milk.

Some things to consider when thinking about milks are the flavor profile and fat content. These two factors offer essential contributions to the final taste and consistency of the milky brew. We found that many times we got better results by combining two different milks, especially for recipes that have subtle flavors. Matcha, for example, seems to get overpowered by coconut milk alone, but when mixed with coconut and cow's milk, the earthy sweetness of the dairy lifts the matcha while the coconut brings gentle tropical brightness to the cup.

It is pretty fun to set up a milk tasting to discover your perfect blend. See the below list for flavor and descriptive information about many different milks.

FULL-FAT COW'S MILK: earthy, sweet, rich mouth-feel

COCONUT MILK: rich, floral, tropical, bright, creamy mouth-feel

ALMOND MILK: subtle nutty taste, slightly sweet, warm

PECAN MILK: creamy, sweet, nutty

OAT MILK: buttery, thick, similar mouth-feel to cow's milk

HEMP MILK: light, mildly nutty

SOY MILK: smooth, flavors range from neutral to citrus or hint of bean

CASHEW MILK: slightly nutty, very creamy

RICE MILK: sweet, thin and watery consistency

MAKING MILKS

Many milks are available for purchase at the grocery store. However, making nut and grain milks at home is a very easy process.

The basics are soak, blend, strain, and drink.

HOMEMADE NUT MILK

1 cup raw, unsalted nuts

2 to 3 cups water for soaking

4 cups water for blending

1 Medjool date, pitted (optional)

$1/2$ teaspoon vanilla extract (optional)

Soak the nuts overnight in 2 to 3 cups water. Drain and discard the water. Blend the nuts, date, and vanilla, adding 1 cup of water at a time, until smooth. Strain mixture through cheesecloth or nut bag. Refrigerate milk, and use within 4 days.

OAT MILK Combine 1 cup oats with 4 cups water and optional date and vanilla. Blend then strain.

HEMP MILK Combine $1/2$ cup hemp seeds with 4 cups water and optional date and vanilla. Blend then strain.

RICE MILK Soak $3/4$ cup uncooked rice with 2 cups hot water for 2 hours. Drain then combine with 4 cups water and optional date and vanilla. Blend then strain.

FROTH

HOW TO HEAT MILK AND MAKE FROTH

Milk is best heated gently over low to medium heat. For creating lustrous froth, the best temperature for dairy milk is 140–150 degrees F. This temperature brings out a delicious sweetness from the milk. Anything hotter and you risk scalding the milk, which creates a burnt and yucky flavor. You know what we are talking about if you've ever had milk that has been over-steamed at a coffee shop.

Once your milk is the perfect Goldilocks temperature, not too hot, not too cold, it is time to make bubble magic. As a side note— not all milks froth the same way cow's milk does. Some of the best alternative milks we have found to froth are almond, coconut, and soy. They are best warmed to about 140 degrees F before frothing. You can do this several ways.

OLD SCHOOL Fill a jar about $^1/_3$ full of milk. Close the jar with a lid and shake. Once foamy, tap the jar a couple times to condense the air in the bubbles and tighten them up. Pour the loose milk into your cup first, holding back the foam with a spoon, then top with your foam.

NEW SCHOOL Get your hands on a whisk. This can be a tiny foam whisk, available online and at kitchen stores, a hand whisk, electric beaters, a blender, or even a stand mixer. Add warm milk and whisk until full and frothy. Like with the jar method, tap your container on the counter a couple times to condense the bubbles, and then pour the loose milk into the cup first. Finally, top with generous scoops of your creamy foam.

ULTRA NEW SCHOOL Use an electric foamer. These are available from kitchen stores and online. You simply pour in cold milk of choice, close the lid, and with the push of a single button, the device heats and foams your milk. It does give you a very consistent foam for each cup. Like with other methods, tap your container on the counter a couple times to condense the bubbles, and then pour the loose milk into the cup first, holding back the foam with a spoon. Top your brew with a cloudy cap of feather-light froth and enjoy.

CHOOSING ADD-INS

ADAPTOGENS & SUPERFOOD POWDERS

In Ayurvedic medicine, warming, soothing milk elixirs have been used for centuries. But now these dreamy drinks are being boosted by healthy, colorful add-ins to reduce anxiety and promote a calming energy. Adaptogens are a group of plants that you can take over a long period of time in order to help your body adapt to stress and other ailments.

One thing to note about most adaptogens is that they have little to no flavor, so they really can be "adapted" to any of your warming bedtime drinks, and they have the added health benefits of calming the nervous system. In our recipes, adaptogens are included in small quantities. However, some of these are powerful if taken in large quantities and over a longer period of time. Please check with your health care provider for any interactions if you are taking medications.

ACTIVATED CHARCOAL This is all the rage with Pinterest and specialty shops around the world—it makes your drink a sexy midnight black and has zero flavor, but its biggest blue ribbon goes to the fact that it is moontastic at removing toxins from your body. Activated charcoal can impact medications. It is best taken 1 to 2 hours before or after any medications. If in doubt, always check with your health care provider.

ASHWAGANDHA Another favorite herb in the traditional Indian or Ayurvedic medicine system, ashwagandha is an energy tonic and soother of nerves. It is excellent for quieting stress and anxiety.

BEET POWDER This intoxicating deep red powder is well known to lower high blood pressure, serve as weight loss support, and provide plentiful fiber and nutrients. It will give your moon milk a range of color from light pink to deep red, depending on how much you use.

It has a slightly earthy flavor and can be used in a wide variety of drinks, including smoothies.

BLUE SPIRULINA This bright blue superfood is an algae known to be high in nutritional value, vitamins, and minerals, and it is a great add-in to create a moon milk moment that is both beautiful and calming to the nervous system. You can buy all of these adaptogen powders on Amazon and have them delivered to your door. They are super easy to use and so fun to try in your milks and other foods. Some can also be found at Suncore Foods: https://suncorefoods.com/collections/superjuice-powders.

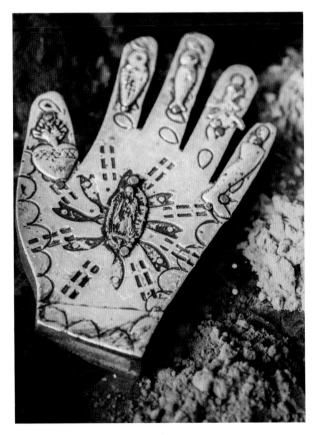

BLUEBERRY POWDER Gentle blueberry powder brings in a soft azure tone, like the first blush of a spring sky. It is packed with antioxidants and helps you look radiant inside and out.

BUTTERFLY PEA FLOWER This beautiful blueish, purplish flower is found in Southeast Asia, is high in antioxidants, has anti-aging healthy skin properties, is flavorless, and makes a beautiful blue drink on its own. But hit it with a little lemon and it will turn bright purple.

CARROT POWDER We use both the ebony carrot and the sun-kissed orange carrot powder in our recipes. Both are full of vitamins A, B1, B2, B3, B6, B12, C, E, and K, in addition to several minerals, including calcium, iron, potassium, phosphorus, and magnesium. This power-packed superfood is easy to find and can be made at home by dehydrating sliced carrots and blending in batches in a spice blender.

ELDERBERRY The gorgeous deep garnet of elderberries is a step into the lush heart of a dark forest. It is a place of quiet dreaming and filled with a juicy treasury of vitamin C, antioxidants, and some immune nourishing properties.

EMERALD PANDAN LEAF The Indonesian green pandan leaf is a new powder on the scene and turns your moon milk bright green. It is known for reducing headaches, oral ailments, and fevers, and has a slight floral taste.

MATCHA Matcha is a Japanese green tea powder high in antioxidants. It calms the mind and relaxes the body, has a distinct nutty flavor, and is bright green in coloration. It does contain caffeine, so keep it in low quantities in the evening and increase the amount if using for a daytime pick-me-up.

PINK PITAYA This electric hot pink superfood powder is just freeze-dried dragon fruit. It is high in fiber and vitamin C and has very little flavor, so it adapts quite well to most flavor profiles.

RAW CACAO Raw cacao is known to be the "food of the gods." It is used in ancient ceremonies to open up the heart and has a natural euphoric compound. It can also improve your memory and boost your bliss. It does not taste like traditional sweetened chocolate and has a bitter flavor, so balancing it with a sweeter component works well here.

ROSE PETALS/ROSE PETAL POWDER Rose petals add an uplifting fragrance and contain vitamin C. They are beneficial for skin, soothe nerves, and can be a gentle heart tonic. Make sure to use culinary-grade rose petals. Dried petals can easily be made into a powder by grinding in a mortar and pestle or herb grinder.

SHATAVARI A long-time favorite herb of Indian traditional medicine, shatavari powder is great for supporting a balanced energy system, calming those frazzled nerves, and tonifying the female reproductive system.

GARNISHES

We feature some truly luscious adaptogenic honeys in this book.

To make, simply combine $^1/_2$ cup of your favorite raw wildflower honey with 1 heaping tablespoon of your favorite adaptogen. For extra sparkle, we added 1 teaspoon of edible glitter. This honey can be used with any of the moon milks or teas. It tastes delicious and looks like unicorn magic!

MAGICAL MARSHMALLOWS

We garnish several of the recipes in this book with delectable, magical marshmallows. These are marshmallows dipped in melted chocolate and sprinkled with edible culinary-grade glitter. We cut them into moon and star shapes.

MARBLED MARSHMALLOWS

String

8 jumbo marshmallows

A selection of your favorite colorful superfood powders

A bag or bowl

Edible glitter

Assorted dried flower petals

Begin by wrapping your marshmallows with the string—try to wrap a few circles around in each direction, perpendicular, horizontal, and diagonal. Next, lightly wet your fingers and dab a little water on the outside of the marshmallow. You do not want to get them too wet. Drop the marshmallow in a bag or bowl with your favorite superfood powder, and then rub the powder into the marshmallow. Let dry for a minute and then cut the strings off. Rub any excess powder into the marshmallow and roll in glitter and dried flower petals.

SWEET SPICED GHEE

MAKES APPROXIMATELY 1 1/2 CUPS

1 teaspoon ground cinnamon

1 teaspoon ground turmeric

1/4 teaspoon ground nutmeg

1/4 teaspoon ground cardamom

1/4 teaspoon ground allspice

3 to 5 strands saffron

1 pound unsalted butter

Add spices to a dry saucepan and heat over medium heat. As you toast the spices, stir them often to prevent them from burning. Once they become warm and fragrant, add all of the butter. As the butter melts, it will begin to separate. Scoop off the foamy milk solids as they rise to the top of the bubbling butter. Once the butter turns golden and smells deliciously nutty and you have scooped off all the milk solids, remove from heat. Strain the melted butter through a fine mesh sieve and store in a clear jar. You can keep at room temperature for up to 1 month or in the refrigerator for up to 1 year.

FLORAL WATER MOONFUSIONS

Why use regular water when you can start a recipe with a mind-fully crafted, superfood-infused splash of hydration? Invite in your highest vibration and a generous beam of gratitude and you will doubly infuse these elixirs with all kinds of beauty.

BUTTERFLY PEA WATER

1 cup water

1 teaspoon butterfly pea powder

Fresh lavender sprigs, to taste

3 things you are grateful for

ROSE AND CALENDULA WATER

1 cup water

1 teaspoon dried organic rose petals (see page 20)

1 teaspoon dried calendula

A heartfelt smile

CHAMOMILE AND LAVENDER WATER

1 cup water

1 teaspoon dried lavender

Fresh lavender sprigs, to taste

1 teaspoon dried chamomile

Fresh Chamomile sprigs, to taste (optional)

A favorite memory

To make, combine the water and herbs in an 8-ounce Mason jar. Give a shake and whisper your words of gratitude to the water. Leave to infuse for at least 15 minutes and up to 1 day. Strain and use in place of water in any recipe, or add as a finishing splash before serving a milk.

DROPPING INTO THE MOMENT

In a media-saturated culture, it's very easy to lose connection with the present moment and the simple pleasures of having real-life conversations with people. We need to take the time to be still and actually just appreciate the moment we are in.

Creating mindful daily practices that can help you feel more positive in your life and more connected to yourself can be simple and incredibly helpful in keeping the vibes high and your energy calm and happy.

We recommend dropping into the moment with your favorite moon milk. Once you start experimenting with these recipes, you will find your favorite flavors and the milks that are most calming for you. We have offered various "mindful moon moments" and simple "moon mantras" with positive affirmations throughout the book to pair with your nightly practice of soothing the soul. You will find that a simple daily expression of gratitude or an acknowledgment of yourself can be reaffirming and calming. Give it try!

BEDTIME SNACK TIPS

Having a light snack or beverage before bed can help you settle into a restful, well-nourished sleep. Moon milks are the perfect preslumber drink. Some top tips for getting the most out of a bedtime nosh are as follows:

KEEP IT SMALL. Small drinks and snacks are easier on the digestive system.

BE INTENTIONAL WITH YOUR SNACK. Turn off screens and distractions and invite your moon milk to deeply nurture you on all levels.

CHOOSE NUTRIENT-RICH FOODS (like the superfoods in these recipes) and receive the sleep-supporting abilities of these plants.

STARLIT
SOOTHERS

MOON MILKS TO INVITE PEACE & TRANQUILITY

MINDFUL MOON MOMENT

———

I blossom into the infinite
beauty of a moonlit rose.

Take a few moments and mindful breaths to tune into the moon. Close your eyes, find your breath, and become aware of the ebb and flow of the waters in your own body. Sink deeper into this connection with your breathing and your awareness. Envision the blossoming of a rose, how the seed never sees the flower, but they are one with each other.

You can sense the moon above you in the sky right now. Feel the magnetic pull rising and falling between you and the moon. Softly become aware of how the moon grows and flows through the passing days and nights, fully embracing the cycle of life, death, and rebirth. The moon teaches us about graceful transitions, the most secret mysteries of the universe, and the rose teaches us to see the beauty intertwined into each of these phases. These truths of being—that the only constant is change, that we can have many lives in one life—are a deep reflection of our experiences as human beings. Keep in your heart that each moment is as sacred as the next. The moon does not weep at the passing days; instead, it sails through each moment a quiet watcher, and the rose is beautiful as the petals fall onto the earth, redefining her existence again and again.

When you are ready to finish spending time with the moon for now, send the moon a smile from your heart, a bow of gratitude, and maybe add a fresh rose to your bedside table as a reminder of how beautiful you truly are.

ALL THE THYME IN THE WORLD MOON MILK

––––––

I find quiet moments to rest
all through the day.

SERVES 2

2 cups milk of choice

1 teaspoon fresh lemon balm leaves

1 teaspoon fresh or dried chamomile

3 sprigs fresh thyme

1 teaspoon maple syrup, or more to taste

Place milk in a saucepan over low heat. Add all the herbs and warm gently. Once it comes to a simmer, place lid on pan and turn off heat. Let milk rest, allowing the herbs to infuse for 5–10 minutes. Strain herbs by pouring milk through a sieve. Add maple syrup before serving.

MINDFUL MILK

―――

I take one step closer to
a peaceful heart.

SERVES 1

1 frozen banana
1 cup chamomile tea
1 teaspoon maple syrup
1 pitted Medjool date
pinch of sea salt
pinch of nutmeg

Blend everything in a blender until smooth. Enjoy immediately as this milk is best when just made.

BALANCE
BREW

My heart is a treasure
I carry with me at all times.

SERVES 1

1 cup organic milk (dairy or alternative)

10 strands saffron thistles

$1/2$ teaspoon shatavari powder (see page 20)

1 teaspoon Sweet Spiced Ghee (page 23)
   (substitute coconut oil for dairy free)

Place the milk in a saucepan and bring to a boil then add saffron.
Remove from heat. Stir in the shatavari powder and add the ghee.
Drink an hour or so before bed.

CALMING CARDAMOM MOON MILK

---

*I spiral into an ocean of
calm tranquility.*

SERVES 2

SPICED CARDAMOM SYRUP

1 ounce whole cardamom pods

5 whole cloves

1 cinnamon stick

2 whole star anise

1 teaspoon dried ginger

$3/4$ cups brown sugar

1 cup water

MOON MILK

2 cups milk of choice

2 to 3 teaspoons Spiced Cardamom Syrup, to taste

1 teaspoon turmeric or reishi powder (optional)

For the syrup, heat all ingredients in a small saucepan over
medium-high heat until sugar has dissolved, stirring constantly.
Take off the heat and let steep, covered, for 1–2 hours. This can be
made ahead and stored in the refrigerator for up to 2 months.

For the moon milk, heat all ingredients in a saucepan over low
heat until hot but not boiling.

MAGIC HOUR

---

*I am bright and shiny and
perfect in my imperfection.*

SERVES 1

1 cup water

1 bag chamomile tea

$^1/_2$ teaspoon honey, or more to taste

1 teaspoon pitaya powder (see page 20)

$^1/_2$ teaspoon vanilla extract

$^1/_4$ cup almond milk

Bring the water to a boil in a small saucepan, add the tea bag, and
steep for 3–5 minutes. Whisk in honey, pitaya powder, and vanilla.
Add almond milk and enjoy. You can also froth this drink using
your favorite frothing method (see page 15).

SLEEPYTIME
CHAI

---

*My mind and heart are open
to receive dreamy messages
and insights.*

SERVES 1

CHAI SPICE MIX

4 tablespoons ground cinnamon

3 tablespoons ground ginger

4 1/2 teaspoons ground cardamom

1 tablespoon ground black pepper (use less pepper for less spice)

3/4 teaspoon ground nutmeg

3/4 teaspoon ground cloves

CHAI

1 1/2 teaspoons Chai Spice Mix

1 tablespoon maple syrup, or more to taste

1 cup milk of choice

For the spice mix, place all of the spices in a small container and shake or stir to combine. Store at room temperature for up to 3 months.

For the chai, combine chai mix, maple syrup, and milk of choice. Blend or whisk together in a saucepan over low heat until hot but not boiling.

BLUSHING
MOON MILK

———

*I move through the world
with grace and compassion.*

SERVES 2

2/3 cup water

3 bags rooibos tea

1 teaspoon sun-kissed carrot powder (see page 19)

2 teaspoons honey

1/2 teaspoon vanilla extract

2 cups milk of choice

Bring the water to a boil in a small saucepan, add the tea bags and carrot powder, and steep for 5 minutes. Remove tea bags then add honey and vanilla. Heat milk in a separate pan on stovetop or use a milk frother (see page 15); add to tea mixture.

MATCHA
BROWNIE

———

*I welcome divine inspiration
into my creative process.*

SERVES 2 TO 3

2 heaping teaspoons matcha powder (see page 19)

1 tablespoon coconut butter

1 tablespoon almond butter

1 tablespoon cacao nibs, plus more for garnish

1 tablespoon raw cacao powder

2 $^1/_2$ cups oat, whole cow's, or almond milk

1 sprig fresh mint (optional)

1 to 2 tablespoons maple syrup, or to taste

Blend matcha, butters, cacao nibs, and cacao powder with $^1/_2$ cup milk until smooth. Place in a saucepan, add the rest of the milk, and heat with the mint, if using, over low heat until hot but not boiling, whisking constantly. Add maple syrup. Remove mint sprig before serving.

SLEEPING
BEAUTY

———

*I am navigating my muse
in my dream space.*

SERVES 2

2 Medjool dates, pitted

2 cups milk of choice

2 tablespoons coconut butter

2 teaspoons blue spirulina (see page 18) or
butterfly pea flower powder (see page 19)

1 teaspoon bee pollen

2 teaspoons vanilla extract

$1/2$ teaspoon ashwagandha powder (see page 16) (optional)

Soak dates in hot water until softened, and then drain. Blend all
ingredients until creamy, then either heat on stovetop or use milk
frother (see page 15). Serve immediately.

MUSING
MANGO

———

*My spirit is free and
I am full of abundance.*

SERVES 2

1 cup diced fresh mango

$1/4$ cup plain yogurt or coconut cream

1 cup coconut milk

1 tablespoon maple syrup

$1/2$ teaspoon cinnamon

$1/2$ teaspoon ground cardamom

Combine all ingredients in a blender. Process until smooth.

HUNGER
MOON MILK

———

*I am always striving to be
the best version of myself;
I continue to rise again and again.*

SERVES 2

1 large banana

1 cup almond milk

1 cup spinach

2 tablespoons almond butter

1 tablespoon raw cacao powder

2 teaspoons vanilla extract

2 teaspoons maple syrup

2 teaspoons blue spirulina powder (see page 18)

Dash of sea salt

Blend all ingredients until creamy. Serve immediately.

ROSE-EARL GREY LATTE

---

*The universe is conspiring
for my greatest success.*

SERVES 1

1 cup water
1 bag Earl Grey tea
1 tablespoon dried rose petals (see page 20)
1 cup milk of choice
Honey, to taste

Bring the water to a boil in a small saucepan, add the tea bag, and
steep for 3–5 minutes. Remove tea bag. Over low heat, add rose petals
to tea and simmer for 5 minutes. Remove tea from heat and strain.
Add tea back to the pan, add milk, and heat until hot but not boiling.
Remove from heat and add honey then froth (see page 15) if desired.

BLUE MOONFUSION

---

*I open to the freedom
of new horizons.*

SERVES 2

$1/2$ cup wild blueberries

3 teaspoons sugar

$1/2$ teaspoon cinnamon

$1/2$ teaspoon cardamom

$1/4$ teaspoon nutmeg

$1/4$ cup cherry juice

1 teaspoon vanilla extract

1 $1/2$ cups milk of choice

Combine blueberries and sugar in a small saucepan on medium-high heat, stirring constantly. Once sugar dissolves, add spices and cherry juice. Let simmer until blueberries are soft and broken down, about 5 minutes. Gently mash fruit then simmer until sauce has thickened. Add vanilla and milk and warm over medium heat, stirring constantly, until hot but not boiling. Serve and enjoy.

KIWI DREAMIN'

My heart is open and
I am full of trust and surrender.

SERVES 2

1 cup vanilla yogurt

1 frozen banana, sliced

1 cup cashew milk

2 kiwi, peeled

1 teaspoon vanilla

Combine all ingredients in a blender. Process until smooth and serve immediately.

NIGHT

OWLS

MOON MILKS FOR THOSE LATE NIGHTS

MINDFUL MOON MOMENT

———

*I invite all my senses
to be awakened and balanced.*

A playful way to invite balance and change the quality of your energy is to experiment with sensory breathing. Imagine you are wrapped in a cozy, soft blanket of your favorite color, or you are smelling your favorite flowers, or sipping your favorite flavors, or listening to a song that moves you deeply, or getting an epic massage. How do you feel? Are there some senses that make you feel more awake? Some that make you feel more relaxed? As a sensory exercise, close your eyes for a moment, and play with wrapping yourself in each color of the rainbow for 3 to 5 breaths. Make a note of which colors feel most soothing and beneficial to you and invite those colors into your life through food choices, clothing, and art.

Awakening the senses allows us to be alive in our own skin. It makes life more luscious, more delicious, and, really, just more vibrant.

MATCHA
MOON LATTE

———

Peace is my heart's truth.

SERVES 1

$1/2$ teaspoon matcha powder (see page 19)

1 teaspoon maple syrup

$1/2$ cup whole cow's milk

$1/2$ cup coconut milk

1 tablespoon coconut oil or Sweet Spiced Ghee (page 23)

$1/4$ cup hot water

Place the matcha powder and maple syrup in your serving mug and mix into a paste. Combine the milks and coconut oil in a saucepan and begin to gently warm—do not boil. Add a little of the hot water to the matcha paste, about a teaspoon to begin with, and stir well. Add the rest of the water, whisking gently until the matcha begins to form its own froth. When the milk mixture is warm, pour over matcha and stir to gently bring together.

You can also froth (see page 15) milk before pouring over the matcha in a true latte style.

GREEN
GODDESS

_____

I am infinitely full of potential.

SERVES 1

1 tablespoon unsalted pistachios, ground into powder

1 teaspoon honey

1 cup milk of choice

1 tablespoon coconut oil or Sweet Spiced Ghee (page 23)

3 to 5 strands saffron

1 teaspoon dried organic rose petals (see page 20)

Ground cardamom (optional)

Mix the pistachio powder and honey into a paste. In a small saucepan, combine milk with the coconut oil and gently warm—do not boil. Once warm, add the pistachio paste and saffron. Allow to infuse gently for 10 minutes. Strain into a cup and garnish with rose petals or a little sprinkle of cardamom.

GOLDEN
MOON MILK

———

My body is my sacred temple.

SERVES 2

1 1/2 cups water

1 teaspoon grated or very thinly sliced fresh ginger

1 1/2 cups milk of choice, warmed

1/2 teaspoon ground turmeric

1/8 teaspoon ground cinnamon

Honey or maple syrup, to taste

Sweet Spiced Ghee (page 23) or coconut butter, to taste

Edible gold stars (optional)

Cayenne powder (optional)

Boil water and ginger in a saucepan for 4–5 minutes. Strain out ginger. In a blender, combine milk, ginger water, spices, and honey. Blend until smooth and frothy. Stir in a dollop of ghee to finish and sprinkle with edible gold stars for extra sparkle. Add a dash of cayenne for a little kick.

SLUMBER SHOTS

———

My heart smiles with joy.

SERVES 2

¹/₂ teaspoon shatavari powder (see page 20)
1 teaspoon dried rose petals, crushed into powder (see page 20)
¹/₈ cup hot water
¹/₂ cup whole cow's milk
¹/₂ cup hemp milk
Rose petals, for garnish

Mix the shatavari and dried rose powders with the hot water to make a paste. Combine milks in a saucepan and gently warm over medium-low heat—do not boil. When the milk mixture is warm, add shatavari paste and whisk well to combine. Pour into 2 small glasses, sprinkle with rose petals, and share with a friend.

STRAWBERRY ELDERFLOWER DREAM

———

*The strawberry moon
shines on all my dreams.*

SERVES 1

1 cup strawberry tea or any fruity herbal tea, warmed

2 to 3 teaspoons Homemade Elderflower Syrup

2 tablespoons milk of choice

1/4 teaspoon vanilla extract

1 teaspoon coconut butter

1/4 cup freeze-dried strawberries (optional)

Use frother (see page 15) or blender to blend tea with elder-flower syrup, milk, vanilla, and coconut butter. Garnish with dried strawberries.

HOMEMADE ELDERFLOWER SYRUP

MAKES 3 CUPS

3 cups granulated sugar

1 3/4 cups water

1 tablespoon plus 2 teaspoons citric acid

15 elderflower heads

1 organic lemon, sliced

Combine sugar, water, and citric acid in a saucepan and heat until sugar is dissolved. Remove from heat and cool to room temperature. Trim the stems from the elderflower heads and discard. Place elderflower heads and lemon slices in large glass jar. Pour cool syrup into jar with the elderflower blossoms. Cover and let steep in the refrigerator up to 48 hours, stirring once daily. Strain the syrup through cheesecloth. Store in a cool, dark place. Keeps for about 4 weeks.

FAIRY NECTAR

———

I invite whimsy into my life.

SERVES 2

2 cups milk of choice
2 teaspoons honey
1 teaspoon vanilla or almond extract
1 pinch ground cinnamon or nutmeg, for garnish

Heat milk, honey, and vanilla in a saucepan until hot but not boiling. Let set for about 5 minutes then pour into 2 mugs and garnish with a sprinkle of cinnamon or nutmeg.

LOVE BREW

_____

All my senses are open to love.

MAKES 1 QUART

$1/2$ cup dried hibiscus flowers

1 cinnamon stick (optional)

4 cups cold water

2 tablespoons to $1/4$ cup simple syrup, or to taste

Lime wedges (optional)

Vanilla milk (optional)

Place hibiscus and cinnamon, if using, in a large jar. Add water. Cover and refrigerate overnight. Add simple syrup to taste, and strain out flowers. Serve hot or over ice with a squeeze of lime or a splash of vanilla milk. Cover and store brew in the refrigerator for up to 1 week.

LAVENDER
HOT CHOCOLATE

I am calm. I am bliss.
I am present in this moment.

SERVES 2

2 cups milk of choice
$1/4$ teaspoon lavender buds
$1/2$ cup premium chocolate chips
Whipped cream, for garnish
Moon-shaped Magical Marshmallows, for garnish (see page 22)

In a saucepan, heat milk and lavender buds until milk is hot but not boiling. Remove from heat, cover, and steep for about 15 minutes.

Strain milk and pour over chocolate chips. Stir together over medium heat until chocolate is completely dissolved. Serve with whipped cream and marshmallow garnish if desired.

ENTER THE NIGHT LATTE

———

I kiss the night
with the mystery of me.

SERVES 1

1 cup almond or whole cow's milk

1 tablespoon maple syrup

1 teaspoon activated charcoal* (see page 16)

1 pinch sea salt

1 teaspoon grated orange zest, plus more for garnish

1 teaspoon dried calendula (optional)

Gently warm milk, syrup, charcoal, salt, and zest in a saucepan over low heat. Once warmed through, froth the milk with frother (see page 15) or whizz in a blender for 30 seconds.

Pour into cup and sprinkle with additional orange zest and calendula petals if using.

*Activated charcoal is best taken 1–2 hours before or after any medications.

MIDNIGHT
REVERIE

———

*I follow the wandering mind
into sweet surrender.*

SERVES 2

BLACK SESAME PASTE

$1/2$ cup black sesame seeds, toasted

$1/4$ cup pitted Medjool dates, soaked in warm
water until soft then drained

$1/4$ cup sesame oil

MOON MILK

2 cups milk of choice

2 tablespoons Black Sesame Paste

1 teaspoon tahini

$1/2$ to 1 teaspoon maple syrup, or to taste

2 teaspoons matcha powder (see page 19) or
emerald pandan leaf powder (see page 19)

Pinch of sea salt

$1/2$ teaspoon vanilla extract

For the sesame paste, in a blender or food processor, combine
sesame seeds and dates. Blend until ground up and gritty. Add oil
and blend until a smooth paste has formed. Store any unused paste
in the refrigerator for up to 1 month.

For the milk, combine all ingredients in a blender and blend until
smooth and frothy. Transfer to a small saucepan and heat until hot
but not boiling.

MAPLE
DREAMIN'

Sweetness infuses my thoughts.

SERVES 1

$1/2$ cup pecan milk
$1/2$ cup oat milk
1 teaspoon maple syrup
1 tablespoon coconut oil or Sweet Spiced Ghee (page 23)
Pinch of nutmeg
Pinch of clove

Combine milks in a saucepan and warm over a medium-low heat—do not boil. When the milk mixture is warm, add maple syrup and coconut oil. Pour into a mug and top with nutmeg and clove.

DANDY
SHANDY

———

Gratitude is a song
my heart sings.

SERVES 1, HOT OR ICED

1 1/2 cups water
1/2 cup almond milk
1 teaspoon coconut oil
2 to 3 tablespoons Dandy Blend (dandelion tea blend)
1/2 teaspoon reishi (optional)
2 to 3 tablespoons maple syrup

Warm the water. Froth milk and oil together using frother (see page 15) or handheld blender and set aside. Place Dandy Blend, reishi, and maple syrup in a mug. Add water and stir to combine. Top with the frothy almond milk mixture.

INTO THE BLUE

———

I invite peace
with each breath.

SERVES 1

1 cup milk of choice, plus extra for frothing

1 tablespoon honey

1 teaspoon blue spirulina (see page 18) or blue
   butterfly pea flower powder (see page 19)

1/4 teaspoon ground cardamom

2 tablespoons toasted unsweetened coconut flakes (optional)

Blend milk, honey, blue spirulina, and cardamom until creamy, and
then heat over medium heat until hot but not boiling. Using milk
frother (see page 15), froth additional milk then top with toasted
coconut if using.

CRUSHED VELVET

I am all things,
and all things are me.

SERVES 1

1 teaspoon beet powder (see page 16)

$^1/_2$ teaspoon activated charcoal (see page 16)

$^1/_2$ teaspoon ground ginger

$^1/_2$ teaspoon vanilla extract

1 teaspoon maple syrup

1 cup whole cow's milk or coconut milk

1 tablespoon coconut oil or Sweet Spiced Ghee (page 23)

$^1/_2$ teaspoon bee pollen

Marbled Marshmallow (see page 22), for garnish

In a cup or mug, add the beet powder, charcoal, ginger, vanilla, and maple syrup and mix into a paste. Warm milk in a saucepan over low heat—do not boil. When the milk mixture is warm, pour over the paste mixture and stir to gently bring together. Froth the milk using your favorite method (see page 15). Stir in coconut oil. Sprinkle with bee pollen, garnish with marshmallow, and sip with joy!

UNICORN
SUNSET

———

Every heart has a little
magic spark to share.

SERVES 2

$^1/_2$ cup carrot juice

1 $^1/_2$ cups almond or coconut milk

$^1/_2$ teaspoon sugar

$^1/_2$ teaspoon dried ginger

$^1/_2$ teaspoon sun-kissed carrot powder (see page 19)

1 bag chamomile tea

$^1/_2$ teaspoon bee pollen (optional)

Combine carrot juice, milk, sugar, dried ginger, and sun-kissed
carrot powder in saucepan over medium heat. Add tea bag and
steep for 3–5 minutes. Strain then heat on stovetop or in milk
frother (see page 15) until hot but not boiling. Top with bee pollen
if desired.

CALMING
CLASSICS

WALKING - FERN

MOON MILKS FOR COZINESS

MINDFUL MOON MOMENT

––––

I am gratitude.
I unspool into the quiet
expanse of evening.

Gratitude is a beam of light in tired, weary moments. It is easy to be jaded or hold tight to wrongs and worries of the day. However, like a soft green fern unfurling in the delicate light of dawn, gratitude unwinds our internal barriers and soothes battered feelings. As Mother Nature gives freely to us, take a moment to give freely to yourself.

Start the practice of finding one small thing to be grateful for in your dark or exhausted moments. This challenge can be the first step toward something better, and, even more importantly, spiritual mastery. Making the time for gratitude will serve your highest good in ways that will give you tangible results.

One easy place to start is to be grateful for the spark of life in your body: You are alive right now, in this moment, and you can choose to be grateful for your breath and the beat of your heart. You could find gratitude for the nourishing foods you get to create, or even the moments of time to nurture your tender heart.

CINNAMON & SUGAR MOON MILK

———

I gather in
contentment and joy.

SERVES 3

3 cups milk of your choice
$1/2$ teaspoon vanilla extract
1 teaspoon brown sugar
1 teaspoon ground cinnamon
$1/4$ teaspoon ground nutmeg

CINNAMON TOAST CRUMBLES
1 piece thick white bread
Butter
1 teaspoon ground cinnamon
1 teaspoon sugar

Combine milk, vanilla, sugar, and spices in a saucepan. Warm over medium-low heat until just simmering; stir frequently. Once warm, pour into cups and top with cinnamon toast crumbles.

To make the crumbles, toast the bread until golden. Spread with butter and sprinkle with cinnamon and sugar. Let cool completely—it's even better to let dry out for about 30–60 min.

Whizz in food processor until it resembles coarse breadcrumbs. Store in a jar and use as topping for moon milks, yogurts, and ice creams.

VERDANT
LUNA

———

*I flow into the limitless energy
of the universe.*

SERVES 1

1/2 teaspoon matcha powder (see page 19)
1/2 teaspoon pandan leaf powder (see page 19)
1/4 teaspoon ground cardamom
1/4 teaspoon ground ginger
1 teaspoon maple syrup
1/2 cup pistachio milk
1/2 cup coconut milk
1/4 cup hot water
1 tablespoon toasted coconut flakes, for garnish
Pistachio nougat or biscotti, for garnish (optional)

In a cup, add the matcha, pandan, cardamom, ginger, and maple
syrup and mix into a paste. Combine the milks in a saucepan and
gently warm—do not boil.

Add a little of the hot water to the matcha paste, about a teaspoon
to begin with, and stir well. Then add the rest of the water,
whisking gently until the matcha begins to form its own froth.
When the milk mixture is warm, pour over the matcha and stir to
gently bring together. Froth in your favorite manner (see page 15).
Garnish with toasted coconut or the nougat.

LET'S GET FIGGY WITH IT

Bliss is found through
new adventures and old friends.

SERVES 1

ROSEMARY SIMPLE SYRUP

1 cup water

1 cup sugar

$1/4$ cup rosemary leaves

MOON MILK

1 cup oat milk

2 tablespoons fig jam or preserves

1 teaspoon rosemary simple syrup

Dash of ground cinnamon

For the syrup, combine water, sugar, and rosemary leaves in a small
saucepan. Bring to a boil, stirring until sugar dissolves. Simmer
1 minute. Remove from heat and let steep for about 30 minutes.
Strain then cool.

For the milk, blend milk with jam then strain into a saucepan.
Add simple syrup. Heat until hot but not boiling. Serve with a dash
of cinnamon on top.

COZY CACAO

I step into hopeful trusting.

SERVES 2

2 cups water

2 rose quartz stones

Pinch of chile or cayenne pepper

1/2 cup raw cacao powder

1 teaspoon ebony carrot powder (see page 19)

2 teaspoons dried organic rose petals (see page 20)

2 teaspoons adaptogenic honey (we like pea flower)

2/4 teaspoon ground cardamom

2/4 teaspoon ground cinnamon

1 teaspoon vanilla extract

Warm the water in a saucepan with the rose quartz in it. The rose quartz invites in the love qualities the crystal embodies. Add the chile just before the water comes to a boil. Add in the cacao powder, ebony carrot powder, rose petals, honey, spices, and vanilla. Using a ladle, remove the quartz. Use a whisk to stir the brew until it's all blended and you get a frothy top. Serve with a spoon or stirring stick to keep the smooth consistency as you drink. The cacao will settle at the bottom over time.

PRETTY IN PURPLE MILK

---

*I am in service
to my highest good.*

SERVES 1

BERRY & LAVENDER PURÉE

1 cup berries of choice

1 tablespoon honey

$^1/_2$ teaspoon lavender buds, plus extra for garnish

Pinch of sea salt

MOON MILK

1 cup milk of choice (whole cow's milk makes
   for an especially lush result)

3 tablespoons Berry & Lavender Purée, divided

To make the berry purée, blend everything together in a blender
until smooth and well combined.

In a small saucepan, gently warm milk over low heat; do not boil.
Add half the berry purée to warm milk. Place the remaining purée
into a cup, gently pour the berry milk over the purée. Give a stir to
bring together and garnish with a little lavender if you like.

NUTS FOR MOON MILK

---

*I practice being present
fully in this moment.*

SERVES 1

1 teaspoon maple syrup

1/4 teaspoon almond extract

1/2 cup almond milk

1/2 cup pecan milk

1 tablespoon chopped Toasted Spiced Nuts (opposite)

Add all your ingredients except the toasted nuts to a pan and warm together. Once just simmering, remove from heat and pour into mug. Top with Toasted Spiced Nuts.

TOASTED SPICED NUTS

MAKES 1 $^{1}/_{2}$ CUPS

1 tablespoon butter
$^{1}/_{2}$ cup almond slivers
$^{1}/_{2}$ cup hazelnuts
$^{1}/_{2}$ pecan halves
1 teaspoon cinnamon
1 teaspoon nutmeg
1 teaspoon brown sugar

Melt the butter in a frying pan over medium heat. Add the nuts, spices, and brown sugar, tossing to coat. Continue tossing and stirring until the nuts brown, being careful not to burn. Take off heat and allow to cool. Store in jar on the counter for 1 week. Also makes a great salad, muffin, and oatmeal topper.

PB & JELLY TIME

———

The innocence of childhood
is a spark in my heart.

SERVES 1

2 tablespoons creamy almond or peanut butter
$1/2$ cup almond milk
$1/2$ cup oat milk
2 heaping teaspoons fruit jam or preserves
Pinch of ground cinnamon

Whisk all ingredients together in a saucepan over medium heat until smooth. Strain if using any seeded berry jams, and serve.

PEACHES
& CREAM

———

*I release the day's worries
and enjoy now fully.*

SERVES 2

1 cup whole cow's milk
$1/2$ cup Warm Peach Compote (page 96)
Pinch of ground cinnamon or ginger for garnish

Warm the milk in a saucepan. Divide the compote between 2 mugs.
Once the milk is warm, pour over the top of the compote. Stir to
combine and garnish with a little pinch of cinnamon or ginger.

WARM PEACH COMPOTE

MAKES 1 CUP

3 fresh peaches, peeled, pitted, and diced
2 tablespoon brown sugar
$1/4$ cup water
Pinch of ground ginger
Pinch of ground cinnamon
1 vanilla bean

Combine everything in a saucepan except the vanilla bean. Simmer gently over medium heat, stirring occasionally. Cut the vanilla bean in half and scrape the seeds into the pan. Let the mixture bubble away for about 15 minutes until the peaches start to break down and the mixture thickens.

MAMA'S
MALTY MOON

———

*I see the many blessings
in my life.*

SERVES 2

2 cups milk of choice
1 vanilla bean
$1/3$ cup malt powder
Pinch of ground ginger
1 teaspoon maple syrup or more, to taste

Place milk in a saucepan. Slice the vanilla bean in half lengthwise
and scrape the small seeds into the milk. Allow to infuse for 5–10
minutes over very low heat. Turn heat up to medium low and
add the malt powder, ginger, and maple syrup. Once everything is
warmed through and combined, you can froth with a small whisk
or simply divide into cups and enjoy.

APPLE PIE
IN THE SKY

———

*My dreams are sweet and
full of possibility.*

SERVES 2

1 cup whole cow's milk
$1/2$ cup Apple-Chamomile Compote (page 100)
$1/2$ cup Apple-Ginger Chai (page 100)
Pinch of ground cinnamon or ginger

Warm the milk in a saucepan. Divide the compote between 2 mugs.
Once the milk is warm, pour over the top of the compote. Using the
back of a spoon, pour the chai in a steady stream down the inside of
the cup. This will create a layer of chai in between the compote and
warm milk. Garnish with a little pinch of cinnamon or ginger.

APPLE-CHAMOMILE COMPOTE

MAKES 1 CUP

2 green apples, peeled, cored, and diced
2 tablespoons brown sugar
Vanilla bean
$1/4$ cup chamomile tea
Pinch of ground ginger
Pinch of ground cinnamon

Combine everything in a saucepan except the vanilla bean. Simmer gently over medium heat, stirring occasionally. Cut the vanilla bean in half and scrape the seeds into the pan. Let the mixture bubble away for about 15 minutes until the apples start to break down and the mixture thickens.

APPLE-GINGER CHAI

MAKES 1 $1/2$ CUPS

$1/2$ cup apple juice
1 cup Sleepytime Chai (page 39) or 1 bag
   chai tea and 1 cup water, brewed

Combine chai and juice together in pan and warm through.

ROSIE CHAI

———

*I stay in high vibration,
even when faced with
personal struggle.*

SERVES 2

2 cups nut milk of choice

1 teaspoon Chai Spice Mix (page 39)

1 teaspoon organic rose petals, plus extra
for garnish (see page 20)

1 tablespoon cashew nut butter

1 teaspoon maple syrup

Pinch of sea salt

Place milk in a saucepan over low heat. Add the spice mix and
rose petals and bring to a simmer. Cover with lid, turn off heat,
and infuse for about 10 minutes. In a blender, add milk, nut
butter, maple syrup, and salt. Process until frothy and smooth. You
can reheat in pan on stovetop if you like to serve warm, or pour
into 2 cups and enjoy it as is at room temperature. Top with an
extra sprinkle of rose petals.

TWILIGHT DELIGHT

———

*I gently slip into the
twilight of soft dreams.*

SERVES 2

2 apricots, pitted and sliced
$1/4$ cup coconut butter
1 teaspoon dried ginger
1 teaspoon bee pollen
1 teaspoon almond extract
2 cups almond milk

Blend apricots with coconut butter, ginger, bee pollen, and almond extract until smooth. Heat the milk in a saucepan until hot but not boiling. Briefly blend until all ingredients are combined and enjoy immediately.

BANANA
BRÛLÉE

I breathe in calm.
I breathe in love. I breathe out calm.
I breathe out love.

SERVES 2

1 large banana
4 teaspoons demerara sugar
2 cups coconut or oat milk
2 tablespoons brown sugar
1 teaspoon ground cinnamon

For the brûléed banana, preheat oven to broil, making sure
the rack is in the top third of the oven. Slice the banana in half
lengthwise, keeping the peel intact. Set the banana, sliced side up,
on a baking sheet. Sprinkle the banana with demerara sugar so
the sugar generously covers the sliced banana. Broil until sugar is
caramelized and golden brown, rotating halfway through, about
5–7 minutes. Remove from oven and let cool slightly. Keeping the
banana in the peel, slice the banana into pieces. Be careful of the
hot sugar. Remove banana slices from peel and place into mugs.

Heat the milk, brown sugar, and cinnamon in a saucepan until
hot but not boiling. Pour over banana slices in each mug to serve. If
you like a smoother texture, blend everything together in a blender
before heating the milk mixture.

ITALIAN
SUGAR CLOUDS

———

I notice all my heart hits.

SERVES 1

1 cup whole cow's milk

1 vanilla bean

1 teaspoon sugar

1 teaspoon vanilla extract

White chocolate-dipped Magical Marshmallows
    (see page 22) (optional)

Place milk in a saucepan over low heat. Slice the vanilla bean in
half lengthwise and scrape the seed into milk. Allow to infuse for
5–10 minutes over very low heat. Turn heat up to medium low and
add the sugar and vanilla extract. Froth the milk so it transforms
into the most glorious cloud. You can use a hand whisk or the milk
frother (see page 15) of your choice. Pour into a cup, holding back
the foam so the milk pours first. Then top with fluffy clouds of foam
and marshmallows to garnish.

Note: Mario DiDanoto created this dreamy recipe and let us use it
for this book. He currently owns a little kiosk in Los Angeles called
Belli Fratelli Roasters.

NODDY
TODDIES

MOON MILKS WITH EXTRA SPIRIT

MINDFUL MOON MOMENT

———

*I embrace my childlike playfulness
and laugh with glee.*

Step into a world of playful unwinding. As you percolate these
precocious potions, choose to be in a whimsical mindset. This might
mean a sprightly addition of winks and sparkles, or the lustrous
shine of a crystal in the punch. Perhaps it is the sprinkle of jubilant
laughter. Laughing has long been known to lift hearts, ease minds,
and reduce stress. And cheery cackling is contagious, its bright
spark kindles the flame of joy from one heart to the next. If you can
simply start laughing—a loud guffaw, a sultry chuckle, or a hesitant
giggle—it is all good. What generates the spontaneous mirth in your
life? How can you nurture and cultivate a garden of merriment?
The answer is as simple as practicing smiling and laughing.

So we invite you now to try it . . . go on . . . sparkle like a crystal
and laugh like you mean it!

LAVENDER HONEY NIGHTCAP

---

*I am a dreamer in the land
of milk and honey.*

SERVES 2

HOMEMADE LAVENDER HONEY SYRUP

1/4 cup dried lavender

1/2 cup water

1/4 cup honey

NIGHTCAP

Ice

2 ounces vodka

2 ounces heavy cream

1 egg white

2 ounces Homemade Lavender Honey Syrup

Fresh lavender blossoms (optional)

For the syrup, place lavender and water in a saucepan and bring to a boil. Simmer until water is reduced by half. Strain lavender then mix warm lavender water with honey until the honey is dissolved. Store in a bottle in a cool dry place until ready to use. Keeps for about 2 weeks.

Fill a cocktail shaker with ice and add all the ingredients. Shake until it is well-mixed and frothy. Strain into 2 glasses and sprinkle with lavender blossoms.

MOONLIGHT MULLED
CHERRY TODDY

———

*I beam like a
radiant celestial being.*

SERVES 2

2 cups cherry juice

2 tablespoons orange juice

$1/4$ cup cherries, pitted and halved

1 orange, sliced into 8 slices

1 teaspoon maple syrup or honey

MULLING SPICES

1 cinnamon stick

1 star anise

4 whole cloves

1 bay leaf

$1/4$ teaspoon dried ginger

Pinch of nutmeg

2 cardamom pods, crushed

Combine cherry juice, orange juice, cherries, orange slices, and maple syrup in a saucepan. Bring to a boil then add mulling spices. Turn off heat and let rest, covered, for about 2 hours to infuse spices. Strain fruit and spice mix, reserving the cinnamon stick for garnish. Heat liquid to drinking temperature, or store in the refrigerator for up to 2 weeks.

TIPSY BLACK FOREST MILK

———

Hold a crystal,
save a life.

SERVES 1

1 cup whole cow's milk or almond milk

1 teaspoon activated charcoal (see page 16)

1 teaspoon ebony carrot powder (see page 19)

1 teaspoon raw cacao powder

1 tablespoon maple syrup

1 tablespoon Cherry Compote (page 116)

1 ounce cherry liqueur

Chocolate dipped and sparkled brownie bites (optional)

Whipped cream (optional)

Gently warm the milk in a saucepan over low heat. Make a paste with activated charcoal, ebony carrot powder, raw cacao, and maple syrup. Use a little of the warmed milk to loosen the paste and then mix completely into the milk, whisking well to combine. Place the compote in a glass. Froth (see page 15) the dark milk and pour into the glass, pouring the milk in first and then topping with foam. Using the back of a spoon, carefully pour the cherry liqueur over the spoon and down the inside of the glass, creating a layer between the compote and milk. Garnish with brownies or whipped cream.

CHERRY COMPOTE

MAKES 1 CUP

2 cups dark cherries, pitted and halved
2 tablespoons brown sugar
$1/4$ cup cherry juice
1 teaspoon ground ginger
1 teaspoon ground cinnamon

Combine everything in a saucepan. Simmer gently over medium heat, stirring occasionally. Let bubble for about 15 minutes until the cherries start to break down and the mixture thickens. Remove from heat and store in a clean glass jar until needed. Keeps up to 2 weeks in the refrigerator.

NOD OFF NOG

———

The warmth of good friends
brings cheer to my heart.

SERVES 6

5 eggs, separated

1 cup sugar

4 ounces spiced dark rum

2 ounces apple or peach brandy

1 teaspoon nutmeg

1 teaspoon ground cinnamon

2 cups half-and-half

1 cup heavy cream

In a mixer, whisk the egg yolks until they are pale and have
increased in volume. Carefully add the sugar, a little at a time, as
you continue to mix. When the sugar is completely incorporated, the
yolks should have a spooling ribbon consistency. Turn off the mixer,
and with a hand whisk, gently fold in the rum, brandy, and spices.

In a separate bowl, whisk the egg whites until they form soft
peaks. Gently fold the egg whites into the yolk base. In another
bowl, whisk the creams together until soft peaks form then gently
fold into yolk base mixture. Transfer mixture into clean jars
with lids and store in the refrigerator for 2–4 weeks. Shake the
jars a couple times a week to keep everything mixed together.

Give the eggnog a generous shake before serving. The curing
process makes the eggnog soft and smooth, with a rich, spiced
fragrance and lush custardy mouthfeel. To serve, pour into mugs
or glasses. This can be enjoyed chilled or gently warmed.

CEREAL MILK & COOKIES COCKTAIL

―――

The night brings rest and renewal to my spirit.

SERVES 4

1 cup frosted cornflakes cereal

3 cups milk of choice

2 ounces Baileys Irish Cream liqueur

2 ounces Frangelico liqueur

1 teaspoon orange zest

Cookies for serving

To make the cereal milk, soak the cornflakes in the milk for about 15 minutes. Strain.

You can serve this drink warm by gently heating the milk and frothing (see page 15) in your favorite way. Evenly divide into 4 cups. In a cocktail shaker, combine the liqueurs. Shake well and strain into the 4 cups. Garnish each cup with the orange zest. You can also serve it as a cold brew: Combine all the ingredients in a large jug. Pour in batches into a cocktail shaker filled with ice. Shake well and strain into a glass, garnishing with orange zest. Either way, serve with your favorite cookie!

HORCHATA
LATTE

———

*I am a sultry expression
of my inner fire.*

SERVES 2

2 cups Horchata (opposite)

4 ounces rum

Pinch of ground cinnamon

Freshly grated nutmeg

To make the cocktail, warm the Horchata in a saucepan. Froth (see page 15) then add the rum. Pour into mugs and top with spices.

HORCHATA

4 cups long-grain rice

8 cups water

6 cinnamon sticks

1 teaspoon ground cinnamon

1 (14-ounce) can sweetened condensed milk

1 (13.5-ounce) can coconut milk

In a large skillet, toast the rice over medium heat, stirring until fragrant, about 25 minutes. Let cool for 45 minutes. Transfer the rice to a large container and cover with the water. Add the cinnamon sticks and let set overnight. After 24 hours, pulse rice and water in a blender—you will need to do it in batches. It doesn't need to be perfectly smooth. Strain the mixture through a nut milk bag or a fine mesh sieve and set over a bowl. Finish the Horchata by blending the strained milk with the cinnamon, condensed milk, and coconut milk. Keep refrigerated until ready to use.

Index

METRIC CONVERSION CHART

VOLUME MEASUREMENTS

U.S.	METRIC
1 teaspoon	5 ml
1 tablespoon	15 ml
¼ cup	60 ml
⅓ cup	75 ml
½ cup	125 ml
⅔ cup	150 ml
¾ cup	175 ml
1 cup	250 ml

WEIGHT MEASUREMENTS

U.S.	METRIC
½ ounce	15 g
1 ounce	30 g
3 ounces	90 g
4 ounces	115 g
8 ounces	225 g
12 ounces	350 g
1 pound	450 g
2 ¼ pounds	1 kg

TEMPERATURE CONVERSION

FAHRENHEIT	CELSIUS
250	120
300	150
325	160
350	180
375	190
400	200
425	220
450	230